Berkhamsted Common, Hertfordshire.

Fresh Air from the Common

When I was boy in Berkhamsted I used to collect our family's meat from the butcher. One hot day he explained how he always kept the back door of the shop open 'to let in the fresh air from the common', which lay a mile to the north. The 3,000-acre tract of wood and gorsy heath (Linnaeus is reputed to have knelt to give thanks for the blaze of furze there) was saved from enclosure by Augustus Smith, a commoner, and the Commons Preservation Society (the original Open Spaces Society) in 1866.

The society had only been formed in 1865, but within a year it was nobly conspiring to throw down Lord Brownlow's illegal fences (see p.5). The action was a turning point in the history of commons. No wonder the place still inspires local people, from butchers to bolshie conservationists: in 1966 the town carnival found more space for 'the Battle of the Common' than for William the Conqueror, whose army pivoted towards London at Berkhamsted in 1066. The common, now largely owned by the National Trust, survives. Its cryptic Iron Age ditches, its orchids, the 400-year-old beech pollards inscribed with poignant messages from Second World War airmen a long way from home – and all that fresh air flowing down into the town – remind us that such things must be fought for, as they still are by the Open Spaces Society.

Catalyst for the Commons Preservation Society

Burnham Beeches, Buckinghamshire. The Open Spaces Society persuaded the City of London Corporation to buy the common in 1880 to protect it as an open space.

The Open Spaces Society has played a vital part in saving millions of acres of land for the public. It started life in 1865 as the Commons Preservation Society.

Commons are a special type of land: on them commoners – persons other than the owner – have rights to collect wood, graze animals or dig peat for instance. They are a survival from the Middle Ages which the public now has the right to enjoy.

Chestnut Walk, Tooting Common, London.

Much of England and Wales was once common, but in the Tudor period land was made into sheepwalks and after about 1700 more was enclosed by parliamentary acts. Land was required to be left for the commoners but little was. In the mid-nineteenth century, the pressures on commons shifted from agricultural exploitation to development, while the population of the expanding cities needed green space for recreation.

At this turning point for commons, the Commons Preservation Society emerged.

In response to the threats to the London commons, parliament established a committee 'to inquire into the best means of preserving for the use of the public the Forests, Commons and Open Spaces in the neighbourhood of London' (the 1865 Committee). George Shaw-Lefevre (later Lord Eversley), founder of the Commons Preservation Society, was a member.

The 1865 Committee took evidence about Hampstead, Blackheath, Barnes, Wandsworth, Tooting, Epsom, Banstead and Hackney Commons, and Epping Forest. The commons were being used for gravel pits, rubbish dumping and the like. Some lords of the manors deplored their inability to deal with these abuses; others hoped that this would enable them to enclose the land.

The 1865 Committee proposed to amend the law so as to prevent any further metropolitan enclosures. Fearing this, the lords of manors of London commons, having failed to persuade the committee that the commoners' rights had lapsed through non-use, began to enclose the commons. This was the catalyst for the creation of the Commons Preservation Society, which held its first meeting at Shaw-Lefevre's offices in the Inner Temple on 19 July 1865.

The society immediately began fighting the enclosures. It identified well-heeled commoners who were prepared to defend the commons in the courts. The cases were promoted locally but under the direction and management of the society's solicitor Philip Lawrence, and later Robert Hunter. They presented their cases in a sequence calculated to secure hearings from the most favourable judges.

Parliament did not act on the recommendations of the 1865 Committee. However, in 1866 it passed the Metropolitan Commons Act which enabled regulation of any common in the Metropolitan Police District and its management by conservators elected by the ratepayers. The consent of the lord of the manor was not necessary for such a scheme but it had to be approved by parliament. The 1866 act greatly reduced the flow of enclosures.

Campaigning for Commons and Commoners

Elan Valley, mid-Wales.

The Commons Preservation Society, dubbed by Shaw-Lefevre 'the people's watchdog', can claim credit for saving Plumstead, Tooting Graveney, Coulsdon and Banstead Commons, Ashdown Forest, the Malvern Hills and many others.

The society played a vital part in rescuing Hampstead Heath and Wimbledon Common. Its greatest battle was for the remnants of Epping Forest, a former royal hunting chase; here, commoners had rights to pasture cattle and pigs, and lop and pollard the trees for winter fuel, and the forest was enjoyed by Londoners for recreation.

The owners started to enclose it and fell trees. Members of the Willingale family of local labourers broke down the fences in order to lop trees in accordance with the custom. They were summonsed before the local justices and fined. Although the money was available they refused to pay and instead did seven days' hard labour.

'William Morris on horseback in Iceland', caricature by Edward Burne-Jones. Morris was an early committee member of the society.

The society raised £1,000 from its leading members for legal action. The society's solicitor, Robert Hunter, discovered that the Corporation of London had common rights over the forest and persuaded it to get involved. The judge, Master of the Rolls Sir George Jessel, found in Hunter's favour and awarded the inhabitants of Loughton £7,000, which was spent on providing a village hall named the Loppers' Hall.

In 1878 the social reformer Octavia Hill and the Revd Hardwicke Drummond Rawnsley (both members of the society's committee and later founders of the National Trust) expressed outrage that Manchester's 'greed for water' would engulf 'one of our loveliest lakes': Thirlmere. The Manchester Corporation Act 1879 allowed the construction of a reservoir there but the society won clauses giving the public the right of access to adjacent common land. These set an invaluable precedent: in the Manchester Corporation Act 1919, which authorised Haweswater reservoir, the society secured access to the commons with a clause outlawing barbed wire. When Birmingham Corporation obtained the right to construct the Elan Valley reservoir (1892), the society won public access under 'the Birmingham Clauses'. These became a model for later cases, e.g. Stanbury Moor in West Yorkshire and Holne Moor in Devon.

Thirlmere, Cumbria.

Direct action by the society

Berkhamsted Common, immediately north of the town of Berkhamsted in Hertfordshire, was in February 1866 owned by Lord Brownlow. His trustees enclosed 434 acres with fences. The society and Augustus Smith, Lord of Scilly, who had rights of common there, decided to exercise the old practice of abatement.

They sent 120 navvies from London by night to pull down the fences. On 6 March 1866 they travelled on a special train which left Euston shortly after midnight and reached Tring Station at 1.30 a.m. Armed with implements, they marched for three miles and by 6 a.m. had felled the railings and left them in neat heaps. Shortly after, Lord Brownlow's agent discovered that the common was no longer enclosed, but by then local people were flooding onto it to enjoy it once more.

The Society's Baby

Mow Cop Castle, Staffordshire.

Throughout the 1880s the enclosure of commons continued. Those campaigning for commons were frustrated because the society was not able to hold land for the public good. Robert Hunter, now a member of its committee, had this in mind in September 1884 when he addressed the National Association for the Promotion of Social Science in Birmingham.

He named 'three distinct perils' facing common land: enclosure by land commissioners; appropriation by industry; and unofficial enclosure by the lords of the manor.

In 1935 the society raised funds for the purchase of Pentire Head in north Cornwall.

'The remedy,' he said, was 'the formation of a corporate company', among other things, to acquire and hold properties to which common rights were attached.

The society published this speech as a threepenny pamphlet. In response, Octavia Hill wrote to Robert Hunter in October 1885 suggesting the name for the company: 'The Commons and Gardens Trust for accepting, holding and purchasing open spaces for the people in town and country'. This prompted Hunter to think up something snappier and all-embracing.

'?National Trust', he pencilled at the top of Octavia's letter. The idea had to wait a decade to come to fruition.

The first meeting to discuss the formation of the new body was held at the society's office at 1 Great College Street, Westminster, on 16 November 1893. The three acknowledged founders of the trust – Octavia Hill, Robert Hunter and Hardwicke Rawnsley (now a canon of Carlisle Cathedral) – with six others met on 16 July 1894 at the Duke of Westminster's Grosvenor House in Park Lane. The trust came into being in 1895 with Hunter as chairman.

The society provided the trust's first office, at 1 Great College Street, and seconded its employee Lawrence Chubb as the first secretary. It also formed local committees which raised money for the trust to purchase threatened land.

The National Trust soon overtook the society in strength but the latter continues to keep a parental eye on its baby to ensure its land and public access to it are in good order.

Mow Cop rescued

Mow Cop Castle (opposite) in Staffordshire is an elevated, romantic ruin standing at 1,091 feet. It was built as a summer-house folly in 1750 and on 31 May 1807 it was the setting for the first open-air meeting of the Primitive Methodists. The society intervened when the castle and surrounding land were threatened by quarrying, raising £400 to restore it as a jubilee memorial to George V in 1935. The National Trust took it over.

This inspired the society to write in its *Journal* of October 1935 that 'No memorial is so enduring as a hill, and a member of the society makes the suggestion that landowners whose territory includes some noble or lovely summit should give directions in their wills for their remains to be interred there … and for the hill and a means of access to it to be given to the public.'

More Space to Enjoy

The sandpit on Horsell Common, Surrey, where the Martians landed in H.G. Wells's 1898 novel *The War of the Worlds*.

At Stonehenge (see box opposite) the society's claim to a right to roam on open country was thwarted, but decades later, legislation gave us the same right on some commons.

The Law of Property Act 1925 gave the public the right to walk and ride on some commons (section 193) and protected many from encroachment and development (section 194). Lawrence Chubb called these two sections 'the coping stones of the edifice which it has taken the society over 60 years to build'.

Section 193 (drafted by the society) gave the public legal access for 'air and exercise' to all commons in the Metropolitan Police District (roughly the area of the former Greater London Council), to urban commons and to rural commons where the owner had made a deed of access.

To help landowners dedicate access, the society prepared model forms and deeds. Under pressure from the society the Crown Estate set an example in 1932 by granting access to its 104 square miles of rural commons in Wales.

Section 194 prevented the enclosure of common land without ministerial consent and gave local authorities powers to enforce against unlawful encroachments on commons. In February 1928 Woking Urban District Council in Surrey lost a case of enforcement concerning a shed on Horsell Common, scene of the Martian landing in H.G. Wells's *War of the Worlds*. The judge considered that the status of that part of the common was not clear. This case highlighted the difficulty of operating section 194 without maps of commons. The society urged the Ministry of Agriculture to undertake a survey but it was not until the Commons Registration Act 1965 that records were established.

Below: The 1,037-acre Town Moor, close to the centre of Newcastle upon Tyne.

Left: A sketch by Georgiana Burne-Jones of William Morris and Edward Burne-Jones taking Philip Burne-Jones on an exeat from Marlborough College. They are driving towards Stonehenge.

Stonehenge shenanigans

When Shaw-Lefevre was head of the Office of Works, after securing the Ancient Monuments Act 1882 he tried to persuade Sir Edmund Antrobus, the owner of the land on which Stonehenge stood, to place the monument under the act's protection. There had been many complaints in the press of damage to the stones 'by visitors or tramps'. Antrobus refused, denying any injury.

He died in 1899 and his son put up a substantial and unsightly barbed-wire fence around the monument, allegedly to protect it from military damage, and charged visitors one shilling to enter. The people of Salisbury and further afield objected and the society raised money to take the matter to court. The attorney-general agreed to adopt the suit, with Shaw-Lefevre, Professor Flinders Petrie (the Egyptologist) and Sir John Brunner (Liberal MP and industrialist) laying the necessary informations.

The case came before Mr Justice Farwell who, unfortunately, ruled in 1905 that the public could not acquire a right to roam (*ius spatiandi*) through prescription, i.e. by roaming for a long period. He went on to say that most of the tracks through Stonehenge were not public rights of way. The attorney-general and the relators lost the case and it cost the society £4,000. Now the National Trust owns the land and English Heritage the stones.

Panorama from Pumlumon, central Wales. This is part of the Crown Estate commons which were dedicated for public access in 1932.

Preserving Public Paths

A 'little winding, quiet byway', Summerheath Wood, Turville, Buckinghamshire.

By the time of its annual meeting on 15 June 1888, the society was moving into the defence of public paths.

Lord (Henry) Thring, first parliamentary counsel, proposed a resolution to approve 'the Bill for the better protection of footpaths and roadside wastes as prepared by a committee of the Society, and introduced in the House of Commons by the Chairman, and that the Society be requested to act as the centre of advice for local footpath societies in relation to the subject'.

Octavia Hill, seconding the resolution, eloquently described how the 'little winding, quiet byways with all their beauty' were vanishing. She concluded that paths 'are a common possession

we ought to try to hand down undiminished in number and in beauty for those who are to follow'.

Hardwicke Rawnsley spoke of battles to save tracks to the summits of Latrigg and Skiddaw in the Lake District, where he wanted the society to take a test case. The resolution was passed unanimously.

Thereafter, the society set up local committees to protect paths in Kent, Surrey, Berkshire, Hertfordshire and Middlesex; and it merged with the National Footpaths Society to form the Commons and Footpaths Preservation

Society in 1899. Local bodies were also created, such as the Wirral Footpaths and Open Spaces Society on the Cheshire coast in 1890.

In 1927 the society became the Commons, Open Spaces and Footpaths Preservation Society. It was not until 1982 that the name was shortened to the Open Spaces Society.

The society was not always on the side of the public. In its *Journal* of August 1928 it complained that it was 'not consulted at any stage in what has turned out to be a most unfortunate attempt to assert a public right of way on foot across Stukeley Park in Huntingdonshire'.

The complexity and uncertainty of the law deterred local authorities from starting legal proceedings. To avoid litigation, the society encouraged the 'friendly settlement of footpath disputes' and established a panel of arbitrators to do this. Astonishingly, the landowners' organisation accepted this, and even more astonishingly, the society's executive committee member Sir Fielding Clarke, arbitrating on a path through the grounds of Amberley Castle in West Sussex, found against the public on the grounds that the estate had been church property.

A 'little winding, quiet byway': Bushey bridleway 68 in Hertfordshire.

Highway verge, Turville, Buckinghamshire. The society's standing counsel, W.R. Hornby Steer, wrote a pamphlet in 1936 on the importance of roadside verges, a cause which the society has championed since its early days.

The society was responsible for the Rights of Way Act 1932, first drafting a bill in 1906. The act enabled members of the public to claim a public path if they could prove 20 years' use without interruption or challenge (as of right). The society encouraged local authorities to carry out surveys of public highways and to record them on maps.

Despite all this immense technical work, the society seemed oblivious to the growing popularity of hiking by people who wanted to escape into the countryside and not become entangled in the law. Thus the Ramblers' Association, formed in 1935 by the coalescence of local and regional federations of clubs, soon eclipsed the legalistic and cautious Commons Society, although the latter remained the principal body concerned with the technical essentials.

The Trespass Saga

Gritstone formations overlooking Kinder Scout, Derbyshire, in the Peak District.

The Kinder Scout mass trespass of 1932 is now a sacred event in rambling circles, but at the time neither the society nor the inchoate ramblers' federations backed it. Five of the trespassers were arrested and jailed. It was falsely alleged that they had attacked and injured keepers.

This was part of the growing movement for free access to the hills, and numerous rallies throughout the 1930s publicised the outrageous way in which walkers were excluded.

The Access to Mountains Act 1939 was badly named. It started out as a useful measure but it was mangled during its passage through parliament, not least because of the furtive work of Lawrence Chubb.

The bill, presented by Arthur Creech Jones (the Labour MP for Shipley), aimed to give the public the right of free access to uncultivated land, subject to provisions preventing abuse of the right. No owner or occupier of such land would be entitled to exclude or bar walkers. However, it emerged that Chubb was working behind the Ramblers' backs to appease landowners.

The Access to Mountains Act 1939 did not provide a general right to roam. Access was to be given by order, made by the minister, on the application of the owner, local authority or organisation representing users. It applied to mountain, moor, heath, down and cliff, in limited circumstances, and was only available during daylight hours. There was a list of restrictions, breach of which would be a crime. Thus mere trespass would have become a criminal offence punishable by fine.

The statutory rules and orders which followed made matters even worse. Anyone wanting access had to pay for the application and much else. The regime was unworkable and nasty.

Yet Chubb persisted in arguing that it was a good thing. In the society's annual report for 1939 he said that the negotiations with landowning organisations 'were carried on in the friendliest spirit, and the society desires to record its deep appreciation of the manner in which the representatives of the landowners endeavoured to reconcile its views with their natural desire to avoid any undue interference with private rights of property'.

He went on to scoff at 'the small but active body of critics who persistently opposed the measure because it did not slavishly follow the impracticable scheme of the original bill'.

By the time of the annual report of 1946 Chubb had the sense to admit that the act was unworkable; fortunately, it never came into operation. The war intervened and the act was repealed by the National Parks and Access to the Countryside Act 1949.

The Lawrence Chubb memorial plaque at Kenwood, Hampstead Heath.

A New Law For the Post-War Era

The Snowdon peaks from the south with the National Trust's Hafod y Llan estate in the distance, Snowdonia National Park.

The National Parks and Access to the Countryside Act 1949 (the 1949 act) had a long gestation. The outcome was a comprehensive piece of legislation addressing both the protection and enjoyment of the countryside.

In 1929 the Labour government appointed the Addison Committee whose 1931 report proposed two types of national park: 'national reserves' which had outstanding scenic and wildlife interest; and 'regional reserves' which were more akin to country parks close to towns. The failure of the subsequent government to pursue this led to the formation in 1936 of a lobby group, the Standing Committee on National Parks, of which the society was a member.

As a result of that committee's pressure, the government commissioned John Dower, an architect and member of the Ramblers' Association, to examine the practical problems, needs and potential of national parks. In 1945 his report recommended ten national parks in England and Wales covering nearly 800 square miles of splendid landscape.

In July 1945 a Labour government came into power committed to the national parks ideal. Within days of taking office, Lewis Silkin, Minister of Town and Country Planning, appointed a National Parks Commission under the leadership of Sir Arthur Hobhouse, chairman of the County Councils Association, to make specific recommendations based on Dower's report. A subcommittee focused on footpaths and access to the countryside.

There was a separate body, chaired by scientist Julian Huxley, to consider the creation of nature reserves – the beginning of a lasting division between conservation and recreation.

The National Parks and Access to the Countryside Act was passed in December 1949. Like the Access to Mountains Act ten years earlier, it was eroded during its passage through parliament so that the final version was considerably weaker than the first. Nevertheless, it covered a lot of ground.

Probably the act's biggest impact on the general public was the requirement that local authorities should produce statutory records (definitive maps) of public paths. In time, lobbying by the society and the Ramblers led to the depiction of definitive paths on Ordnance Survey maps.

Within a decade of 1949, ten national parks in England and Wales were designated. The access clauses once again proved a disappointment. The surveying of potential access land and its opening to the public were left to the local authorities. Very few of them did anything about it.

The 1949 act's main provisions were:

- a National Parks Commission, for the preservation and enhancement of natural beauty in England and Wales, and the provision and improvement of opportunities for open-air recreation;
- national parks, areas of outstanding natural beauty and national nature reserves;
- for public rights of way to be formally mapped and managed;
- long-distance routes (now known as national trails);
- improved public access to open country.

The Last Reserve of Uncommitted Land

Dartmoor ponies on Litcham Common, Norfolk.

The most pressing job for the voluntary sector was now to claim public paths for the new definitive maps. While the Ramblers organised coachloads to survey paths in thinly-populated countryside, the society staidly focused on the legal elements, issuing technical advice on how to claim paths.

Secretary Humphrey Baker published a booklet for local councils. R.V. Vernède, the assistant secretary, wrote a series of articles in the society's *Journal* explaining the rights-of-way survey, reporting progress and reminding readers that the society had long advocated surveys to remove uncertainty about rights.

The first definitive map was published in 1956, by Durham County Council. Even today national coverage is not quite comprehensive.

The 1949 act had failed to deal with commons but the society continued to champion their cause. Commons were threatened by the intensification of their agricultural productivity; the society pressed the Ministry of Agriculture to undertake a broad, high-level investigation.

In July 1955 the government announced a Royal Commission on Common Land charged 'to recommend what changes, if any, are desirable in the law relating to common land in order to promote the benefit of those holding manorial and common rights, the enjoyment of the public, or, where at present little or no use is made of such land, its use for some other desirable purpose'.

The commissioners travelled through England and Wales for 18 months, gathering evidence – from 156 organisations, 97 individuals, 61 county and 81 county borough councils.

The society prepared its evidence early and publicised it to garner support. It recommended management schemes and strong and representative committees to ensure the better use of commons. Public access was to be part of the scheme, and the status of commons was to be preserved to prevent enclosure. The society advocated a commons commission to approve schemes.

The society was the first non-government body to present evidence to the commission, taking two days to do so. When the report was published on 18 July 1958 the society was pleased because many of the recommendations chimed with its proposals. This was the start of a new era for commons.

The cover of the 1951 Country Code.

The Royal Commission on Common Land proposed legislation to achieve the following:

- county and county borough councils in England and Wales to become the commons registration authorities;
- all commons, their rights and owners to be recorded on registers held by these authorities;
- commons commissioners to be appointed to determine disputed registrations;
- the ownership of unclaimed commons to be vested in the public trustee;
- land which is common at the passing of the act to remain common. No enclosure of commons except for compulsory acquisition in accordance with special parliamentary procedure;
- enclosure and other acts to be repealed;
- all commons to be open to the public as of right ('anything less than this would not prove satisfactory,' said the commission);
- any owner or commoner or local authority to be able to promote a scheme for managing and improving commons;
- town and village greens to be registered.

Commons are 'virtually our last uncommitted reserves of land' – Nature Conservancy's evidence to the Royal Commission on Common Land.

Commons Registration

Northam Burrows, common land in north Devon.

The Commons Registration Act 1965 dealt with only one element of the Royal Commission's package: the registration of commons and greens. Ministers promised second-stage legislation to address management and access. However, despite continued pressure from the society, this was not forthcoming for nearly 50 years.

The 1965 act allowed only three years for the registration of common land and its rights and owners (2 January 1967 – 2 January 1970), and the available time was curtailed by a foot-and-mouth epidemic. In early 1966 a conference, organised and led by the society, agreed to form a Central Committee on Commons Registration (CCCR) to deal with registration problems and to set up a documentary research service. Various outdoor organisations were involved. Dr Brenda Swann, a left-wing activist, was appointed as research secretary under the aegis of the society and funded by subscriptions from the CCCR's members.

The society's secretary, barrister Ian Campbell, produced a how-to-do-it guide to the process, and later published the first of the society's many booklets on commons, *Commons registration: a guide*.

Alan Mattingly (then a geography undergraduate at Cambridge and later secretary of the Ramblers, 1974–98) was employed to gather evidence for registration. Among many others,

Richard Harland in North Yorkshire did sterling work. The act said that if land was not registered by the closing date it ceased to be common. There was little time for accuracy; every likely patch must be given a chance. As a result, some land which was not common was registered, but far more was wrongly omitted.

Even after the commons commissioners had spent many years resolving disputes, the registers were inaccurate, inadequate, inconsistent between registration authorities and sometimes incomplete. These problems only began to be remedied by the Commons Act 2006.

Catching the Rye

Wycombe Rye is a 68-acre public open space on the east side of High Wycombe, Buckinghamshire, extending beside the River Wye. Since 1927 it has been owned by High Wycombe Borough Council, now Wycombe District Council.

In 1962 part of the land was threatened with a compulsory purchase order to enable an inner relief road to be built across it.

The society firmly backed the newly-formed High Wycombe Rye Protection Society. The road had already been approved but there was a further inquiry into the appropriation of 2.4 acres of open space. On the inspector's recommendation, the minister confirmed the appropriation order, under the Acquisition of Land (Authorisation Procedure) Act 1946, on 5 February 1965. Since no land was offered in exchange, the order became subject to special parliamentary procedure. This meant that objectors could petition parliament and present their case to a joint committee of both houses.

Both societies gave evidence. Magnificently, the committee ruled that the orders be annulled. The Rye has remained intact to this day.

This is one of countless examples of the society helping a local pressure group to save open space or public paths. Professional expertise, local knowledge and enthusiasm are a powerful mix.

Commons have always been misunderstood; the name implies public or no ownership, but all commons have an owner, even if that person or body is not known. Or the name is confused with the House of Commons, as a policeman joked when the Commons Society used to meet at the Palace of Westminster: 'I can never understand why you lot want to preserve this place.'

Wycombe Rye, Buckinghamshire.

A New Deal For Commons

Hazeley Heath common in Hampshire. In 1981 the landowner sold the lordships of the manors of which this land was part and then claimed that the land was no longer 'waste of a manor'. The Law Lords ruled in 1990 that the land was still waste of a manor and therefore common land. This judgment saved many other commons from deregistration.

The Commons Registration Act was poorly drafted, so it was not long before landowners learnt how to exploit its loopholes. For example, if no common rights remained over a piece of land – perhaps because the owner had bought them – it could be deregistered and used for private purposes.

The commons registers made legal rights visible. In 1989 the Countryside Commission (the National Parks Commission's successor) produced a pamphlet showing that three-quarters of English commons had no more than one right and were at risk. The enclosure movement was reborn and there were cases in the courts.

The society continued to press ministers to enact the promised second-stage legislation (see p.18), but to no avail. In June 1983 it convened a conference to discuss the future of commons. The concluding speakers – Chris Hall (a committee member of the Open Spaces Society and of the Ramblers' Association) and John Cripps, former Countryside

Fur Tor, common land on Dartmoor.

Commission chairman – called for a concordat on commons. The Countryside Commission took up the gauntlet and later that year formed the Common Land Forum, with ministers' blessing. The aim was to sort out the muddle in the existing laws and if possible reach a consensus of all the interests. Ministers rashly promised to legislate should the forum reach agreement.

After two and a half years of tough negotiation, under the wise chairmanship of Maurice Mendoza (a former civil servant), the forum published detailed proposals for legislation. It was an unprecedented consensus of diverse bodies ranging from the society and the Ramblers' Association to the Country Landowners' Association and National Farmers' Union.

So the forum had fulfilled its ambition, and now it was the government's turn to act. However, the government procrastinated.

It consulted the public on the proposals, but the Country Landowners' Association reneged on the forum's agreement. Then the Moorland Association was born to represent wealthy grouse-moor owners, much of whose land was common. The Countryside Commission tried to broker an agreement between the moorland and access organisations without success.

Meanwhile, the government continued to talk of legislation without doing anything. Eventually it broke its promise when the environment minister, David Trippier, announced on the last day of the parliamentary session in July 1990 that commons issues should be resolved locally and there should be no general right to roam. Thus he smashed to pieces the forum's hard-won consensus and gave in to the grouse-moor lobby.

It was to be another ten years before there was legislation for access, and another 16 before management was addressed.

The Common Land Forum recommended:

- an end to wrongful deregistration of commons;
- management schemes with a right of public access and promotion of good husbandry;
- management committees with a balance of interests;
- a duty on local authorities to deal with unlawful encroachments;
- commons with no known owner to be vested in local authorities;
- a right of recreation on village greens with local councils having powers to manage or acquire them where irreconcilable disputes arose.

Action All Fronts

The path through Andrew Lloyd Webber's hamlet of Sydmonton, Hampshire, which the society helped to save in 1996.

The Open Spaces Society has never aspired to be a large or complex body. It moves fast, without bureaucratic constraints.

For most of its existence it has been led by lawyers, but when Paul Clayden left in 1984 the committee appointed a campaigner – Kate Ashbrook, aged 29.

For 20 years (1989–2009) the Dorset historian Rodney Legg served as chairman of the society and as a member of the National Trust's council.

Rodney enjoyed stirring up the National Trust. He argued that it should publicise all its holdings on Ordnance Survey maps and buy land rather than stately homes. By the time Rodney retired from the trust's council in 2010 he had succeeded in getting much trust land opened up and had gained respect from the council and staff.

The path to Morfa Beach, Neath Port Talbot. The society's local correspondent in South Wales helped to save this in 2013.

Since the society has no branches it has not historically had representatives on the ground. In 1985 it formalised its loose arrangement of local correspondents, establishing guidelines and inviting members to apply for the voluntary role. Each candidate is interviewed and vetted to ensure he or she can be trusted to act solo. The correspondents are then free to respond to all the proposed path changes in their areas in accordance with tough guidelines – which are to object to path changes unless there is a clear public interest in the proposal. With only 40 or so correspondents, the society has never had full coverage of England and Wales.

The society prides itself on going where others fear to tread. The result has been some high-profile stories. The following were in the society's sights because of blocked paths or unpleasant path diversions: Nicholas Ridley (when Secretary of State for the Environment); oil magnate John Paul Getty II (Buckinghamshire); film producer David Puttnam (Wiltshire); composer Sir Andrew Lloyd Webber (Hampshire); guitarist Keith Richards of the Rolling Stones (West Sussex); the Rothschilds (Buckinghamshire); industrialist J.C. Bamford (Staffordshire); the Earl Spencer estate (Northamptonshire); and Eton, Harrow, Oundle and Uppingham public schools, to name a few. But most of the society's objections were to unknown landowners and farmers.

In the 1990s the Ramblers revived the campaign for freedom to roam on open country, with the society's wholehearted support. Eventually, in 2000 the Labour government passed the Countryside and Rights of Way Act, giving access on foot to mapped areas of mountain, moor, heath, down and registered common land. The act required the public to claim areas of access land and the society, as it had done in the past for paths and commons, encouraged its members to do so.

Rodney Legg set a fine example by claiming more than a square mile of access land in Dorset and Somerset. But there were many disappointments: much downland was omitted because it was given an impossibly narrow definition.

Access was subsequently extended by the Wales Coast Path in 2012, while the Marine and Coastal Access Act 2009 is creating a path and adjoining spreading room around the English coast.

The first land to be dedicated voluntarily for public access under the Countryside and Rights of Way Act 2000, at Bushey in Hertfordshire, in 2001.

Managing the Commons

Esk Gorge in the Lake District.

Well into the new millennium, commons management, the third element of the Royal Commission's recommendations, had still not been addressed.

English Nature, successor to the Nature Conservancy Council, had a target set by the government to ensure that 95 per cent of all sites of special scientific interest (SSSIs) were in favourable or improving condition by 2010 – and it wasn't making much progress. Since more than half of land designated as SSSI in England is common, it made sense to sort out the management of commons in order to achieve English

Nature's target. There needed to be a system to enable commons to benefit from European agri-environment money.

This was the driving force behind the Commons Act 2006, which provides for commons councils to be established to manage their commons and receive agri-environment money. It also allows for the updating and correction of common-land registers, and a new, improved process

for approving works on commons. The society was pleased that the act allowed the public to take enforcement action against unlawful works, but disappointed that, despite its efforts, local authorities were not given a legal duty to take action (as they have to on public rights of way).

At the start of the millennium, the society was becoming increasingly concerned about the enclosure of commons for alleged nature-conservation reasons. English Nature, the Countryside Council for Wales and wildlife trusts wanted to graze livestock on commons, particularly those where no rights were exercised, to improve biodiversity. However, they did not consult properly and there were some fiery public inquiries with feelings running high.

In 2003 the society met the chairman and director of English Nature, and from this encounter came the idea of developing a protocol for consultation and involvement when managing commons. This was produced by the society, English Nature, the Countryside Agency, the Department for Environment, Food and Rural Affairs (Defra) and the National Trust. Called *A Common Purpose*, it was subsequently adopted by Defra as official guidance. Anyone applying for consent for works on a common was expected to have followed the process set out in *A Common Purpose* before submitting the application. The society then developed the thinking by producing *Finding Common Ground*, which advises land managers on how to gauge and embrace the public interest in commons.

The National Trust sought the society's involvement as it developed its own protocols for staff for its commons, for

Above: Romney sheep and shepherd at Morte Point, North Devon.

Left: Warning signs light up when motorists are travelling at more than 40mph in the North York Moors.

there had been controversy in the past. In recent years there is much better understanding of the need to involve all parties in plans for commons because commons cover so many interests.

A problem is the many small, scattered commons in lowland areas where common rights have been abandoned and the commons are disappearing under scrub. No one wants to graze animals on them because the unfenced roads across them have become rat runs. The society advocates a speed limit of 20mph on unfenced roads across commons and the reintroduction of shepherding. It considers that fencing, reminiscent of the enclosure movement and symbolic of oppression, must be a last resort.

The Threat to Greens

Whomsoever Lane, Bushey, Hertfordshire, claimed by society members and recorded on the official map in 1992. Countless paths must be claimed ahead of the 2026 cut off or they will be lost.

Village greens were originally small areas where local people played games. The Commons Registration Act 1965 defined them as, among other things, land on which local people had enjoyed informal recreation 'as of right', without challenge or permission, for at least 20 years. Village greens are protected from development by laws dating from the nineteenth century.

Traditional greens range from those in village centres, used for cricket and other sports, as at Ockley in Surrey and Finchingfield in Essex, to expanses at Melmerby and Dufton in Cumbria, Barrington in Cambridgeshire and Hamersterly in County Durham.

Many greens were not registered and lost their status, even though they had been used for recreation immemorially. However, 20 years after the registers were closed it once again became possible to register greens. So in 1990 the society began promoting this activity with some success.

Predictably, landowners and developers challenged the process and there has been a succession of court cases analysing every bit of the village greens definition. With support and advice from the society and its book *Getting Greens Registered*, people have registered land which may not conform to the traditional idea of a village-centre green. Ponds, beaches and scruffy plots can all be greens and can make a difference to people's lives.

Traditional village green at Cavendish, Suffolk.

In 2013 the coalition government gave in to developers and changed the law in England. It claimed without evidence that people were abusing the greens registration process in order to stop development. Now, despite the society's strenuous opposition, the Growth and Infrastructure Act 2013 in England outlaws the registration of land as a green if it is threatened by development.

Path law is changing too. Since the Wildlife and Countryside Act 1981 took effect, the claiming of public highways has been a continuous process, with surveying authorities (county and unitary councils) having a duty to keep definitive maps up to date. The authorities have always had backlogs of claims. Paths were blocked or lost under development because, until they were mapped, the authorities did not accept that they were public highways.

As an unfortunate quid pro quo to landowners for the limited freedom to roam in the Countryside and Rights of Way Act 2000, the government introduced measures to cut off the definitive maps to certain historic path claims on 1 January 2026. The promised funding to get the maps up to date was not forthcoming and in 2008 the government's adviser Natural England set up a stakeholder group representing landowners, local authorities and users to reach agreement on how this could be resolved.

With echoes of the Common Land Forum, the group was meticulously chaired by Ray Anderson, a former civil servant. He achieved agreement between traditionally warring parties. After two and a half years the group accepted the cut-off subject to measures to speed up and streamline the claims process; they submitted the package of measures to ministers with a request for legislation.

Above: Traditional village green at Downton, Wiltshire.

Below: Village green at Penpedairheol, Hengoed, Gelligaer, Caerphilly, registered in 2003.

The Future

Kingsmead Field, a valued but threatened open space near Canterbury in Kent.

The slopes of Mount Fuji in Japan are comm

Deccani sheep on common land in Andhra Pradesh, India.

Despite its solid history of campaigning, the society has not, unfortunately, done itself out of a job.

The society has adopted a mix of methods to champion its cause: direct action, as at Berkhamsted Common in 1866; drafting legislation, such as the Rights of Way Act 1932; court action, whether adversarial or friendly to establish a legal principle; lobbying; publicity; and, nowadays, social media. It has been enormously fortunate having access to top lawyers throughout its existence, from Robert Hunter in the early days to George Laurence QC and Jerry Pearlman LLB today.

Common land, in a strictly legal sense, exists only in England and Wales, but common resources are present all over the planet: they may be land, water, air, knowledge or the internet. Today, the society is part of a growing campaign to defend global commons and to help communities worldwide to protect and nurture their common resources.

In Britain we follow our dream of a land where everyone has open space close to their home, every public path is recorded and protected, and our commons are well managed and in good heart. At the society we rely on the generosity of our members and supporters to enable us to continue the crusade we started 150 years ago. Please join us so that our vital work will continue to flourish.

You can join the society at http://www.oss.org.uk/saving-our-green-spaces/ or contact the office at 25a Bell Street, Henley-on-Thames, RG9 2BA. Tel: +44 (0)1491 573535.